Earthbou

Sharon Salisbury O'Toole

Additional Praise for
Sharon Salisbury O'Toole's *Earthbound*:

"With the same precision she uses when counting lambs using a three generations-old abacus of tally beads, Sharon O'Toole reflects on her ranch life in *Earthbound*. This is a rich collection of poems that take you to the land and into her family culture—her mother's kitchen and a Red Desert sheep camp. Every word in this collection comes from personal experience, and that authenticity is inspiring."

Candy Moulton,
Executive Director, Western Writers of America
Author *of The Handcart Migration:*
Neither Tounge nor Pen Can Tell the Story
(Note: incorrect spelling of tounge is correct in book title.)

****

"Delve deep into a profession hidden from mainstream, written with beauty, grit, and grace. In a world of indifference, these poems invite the reader to become intimate with a diminishing lifestyle: six generations defining a passion for the land, livestock, and family."

Patricia Frolander, Wyoming Poet Emeritus
Author of *Married Into It*

****

"Life's true treasures surround us but only with diligence and sensitivity can we know them. Expressing them is the work of poets and artists. I have watched Sharon O'Toole grow as a poet and applaud these treasures she shares with us."

Hal Cannon
Founding Director, Western Folklife Center

Earthbound

Sharon Salisbury O'Toole

Earthbound
© Sharon Salisbury O'Toole 2019

All rights reserved. Red Dashboard LLC Publishing
retains right to reprint. Permission to reprint stories or poetry
must be obtained from the author.

ISBN-13: 978-1-970003-43-7

Book design © Red Dashboard LLC
Cover Artwork © Teresa Jordan
www.teresajordan.com

Published by:
Red Dashboard LLC Publishing
Princeton NJ 08540
www.reddashboard.com

Earthbound is dedicated to my family.

My parents, George and Laura Salisbury,
instilled in me a love for the land (Dad)
and the written word (Mom).

My husband, Pat, and my children and grandchildren
are patient when I say,
"Leave me alone! Can't you see I'm writing a poem!"

Table of Contents

The Landscape

'Round the Campfire

Earthbound

This spring my heart, these rocks my bones,
this earth my flesh, this river blood.
My roots reach down, embrace the stones.

This whetstone land, how fine it hones
my roughened edge, smoothed as I stood.
Heart's well-spring, these rocks my bones.

I heard the croons of ancient crones:
This land your soul, from sky to mud.
Roots reach down, embrace the stones.

You give your all, it only loans
all you need, sustaining food,
your well-spring heart, your rocky bones.

My sighs and laughter, wind entones,
this rain my tears, these streams my blood.
My roots reach down, embrace the stones.

My heart-strings strum its throbbing tones
with wind and water, earth and wood,
with well-spring heart, with rocks my bones.
My roots reach down, embrace the stones.

THE CRITTERS

Abacus

99, 100, slide.

The smooth worn bead
along the leather strap,
another lamb runs by.
Wooden beads worn glassy
by the hands of my grandfather,
my father,
and me.

The leather lace
cut from the hide
of a cow long dead—
supple with oil from
generations of hands.

Beads—yellow and tan,
carved from the hearts of
sarvisberry bushes
by the careful hand of a craftsman
also long dead.

An ancient abacus
counting out spring lambs
as they shoot through the run.
The government requires numbers
if they graze the Forest grass.

Ewes and lambs.
Beads and leather.
Generations of hands on
old tally beads.

99, 100, slide.

Cora

So I look at this pup,
fat with milk and mother's love,
and think, "Maybe"—
maybe this is the one."

Forty-four years with a dog
at my side, a shadow.
Except now. Her Mom, Sadie
likes me well enough.

But she adores Pat
and has the best
Border collie disposition.
She loves to work—

Prefers sheep—they likely
won't kick her across the corral
or turn back to hook her
if she's too close to a calf.

Sadie lays around
when it's time to lay around—
no herding the horses or
chasing the bum lambs.

Gramps, the dad
is almost a pup himself,
still goofy, but smart—
Happy-go-lucky

From a famous line.
these tri-color babies
are his first.
We have high hopes.

So I study this pup—
perfect collar,
black mouth.
Maybe she's the one.

Counting Cards in Las Vegas

Counting cards in Las Vegas
can't be tougher than counting sheep
through a gate on the Red Desert—
not many gates here, but the BLM
wants a tally. Our hand is spread.
My crew shuffles, deals with practiced skill.

The ewes duck past me, kicking up dust.
I slip back and forth, subtle shifts—
a slow waltz guiding the fine-tuned
flow of wooly bodies, heavy with lambs
past my reckoning eye, my arcing hand,
murmuring "one," or "two," or "six."

Stepping just so. to sluice a thin stream
of countable ewes. If crowded too hard,
they stop. I slide away, willing them forth.
Step back too far, and a mob descends,
confounding my tally, making me guess.
"That was about ten."

I watch for the ewe who blindly leaps,
and ignores my living, breathing, waving self.
I don't want to be flattened.
I don't want to lose my count.
A small shout, a flash of the hands,
a mental lock on the number.

She dodges by, number sixty-eight.
then sixty-nine, seventy, seventy-one.
almost fourteen hundred crowd behind,
all intent on piling through that gate
Not One At A Time. Migration's call
urges them onward—green grass fever.

No tally beads. I fold my fingers, one down
for every hundred, after five, one up
for every hundred. The zen of counting
makes it easy for the abacus mind to drift
away from the number, but the rhythm goes on
and the sum stays accurate, or at least close.

They surge, I skip, my crew dances too,
keeping them coming one at a time
through the gate, one and one and one,
on to the shearing shed, on to spring pasture.
We're betting on the come—
but harder to count than cards in Las Vegas.

Branding Reverie

Sweating snorting horses nose through a dusty path—
pursue those darting legs, a nervous slick hide calf.

Studious, squint-eyed roper shakes out a snaky loop—
sails it out for two hind feet, a hissing missile swoop.

Tussling, muscled boys shoot forward with a squirt—
grab that sturdy calf, twist it squirming to the dirt.

Duck that snapping rope, dodge those saber hooves—
shake loose the clinging loop, slide clean with practiced moves.

Shiny magic vaccine shoots in beneath the hide—
a modern incantation, an amulet inside.

A pawing brawling mama makes her presence known—
stomp her calf's tormentors, tear them hide from bone.

The branding man steps in with his irons straight from hell—
sizzling, searing, glowing, a puff of burnt hair smell.

A knife red-stained with blood, sharp as a guillotine,
slices ear and ball sack, motions swift and clean.

Iridescent testicles, young bullhood gone awry,
gives lurking smirking cowdogs their testosterone supply.

A wrist's quick twist takes hornbuds, no headgear for this steer—
eyes all meet, heads all nod, release him from his fear.

Run back where mama's waiting, glaring, blowing phlegm.
They dart into the fluid herd, anonymous again.

Bottle Baby

She was a fine ewe
with a crackerjack lamb.
wintered on the Red Desert,
found a buck,
followed the truck for corn,
gave up her fleece,
made the long trail
down the Atlantic Rim,
gave birth in Loco
kept her lamb right with her,
dodged coyotes, eagles, crows.

When the band trailed out
for summer country
I found her curled
against the cattle guard,
lamb right there.
She looked with wise eyes,
udder ruptured,
flies at her
laying eggs.
Plenty there for
maggot babies.

I snagged her lamb,
hog-tied him on the flatbed,
called the neighbor,
"Would you please come
and shoot her?
No pistol in this pickup,
I can't stand to leave her
eaten alive."

My knot came loose.
That lamb rode unfettered
all the way home.

Raven Musings

I cast about my clever raven gaze—
still, except
to swivel my head and look.
A scavenger life—it's not easy
to make a living every day.

Garbage is good—a feast
to fill the belly—
easy peckings.
Dog food. It's a balanced diet
except they bark so,
chase after me.
Ha! As if they could fly.

Eggs are the best.
Fat slow sage hens
flap up and try
to draw me away.
What do they think—
that I'm a coyote?

Songbirds try to hide
their tiny eggs
from my raven eye.
Ha! Only a snack,
quick but tasty.

Those newborn lambs—
now there's some bang for the buck,
Good luck for my beak.
I seek those napping babies
sated from the first suck
of mother's milk.

Land, hop, outsmart
those big white canines.
Coyote thinks he's clever—
but he alarms the dogs.
Not me. Ha!

A swift peck to the eye,
a stiletto to the brain,
quick as a wink,
that woolly baby disemboweled.
I spy with my raven eye—
dinner.

Trickster, indeed.
Caw! Caw!

Teresa, Dead Today

Well, it's been a hellofaday.
Who knew?
Breakfast at the cookhouse—
all the sheepherders have cellphones now,
DVD's, solar panels,
...but I digress.

A call—
"Mi caballo es muerto,"
dead on the highway—
hit and dead.
Funny," I think, "no call about a wreck...
maybe a logging truck,
construction equipment—
lots going on in the Forest
besides grazing."

So we go, and there,
right on the highway,
dead horse,
broken to bits,
guts wrapped around her belly,
legs torn away.
Teresa.

We raised her from a colt,
trained her to the saddle,
the pack saddle,
the horse trailer.
A good honest mare
on the road at night.
No moon.

Eduardo picketed tomorrow's mount,
left Teresa to graze.

The young father
didn't even see her.
Dark horse, dark night.
smashed his car—
didn't know what he'd hit.
An elk maybe.
All airbags deployed,
a horse head through the windshield,

Then gone, tossed aside.
Blood everywhere,
but hers, not his.
He walked.
We didn't know—
dead horse,
wrecked car,
No report,
no sign of the driver.
I called the deputy.

"We don't know what happened.
There's nobody here—
but two child seats in the back,
glass and blood everywhere.
I think it's horse blood."

Our neighbor stopped.
"I can use her for bear bait."
Well, that's something.
Thank God—no loss
except the car,
and Teresa.

So Cold

Frost mists rise from man and beast,
our crystal breath, ice and steam
puffs ephemeral, path of least
resistance—a ghosting stream.

We push forward, crunch and huddle
through crackling snow, we shove and hunch
through paneled gauntlet, icy muddle
of baaing, milling sheepy bunch.

They know warmth in woolen garb,
We too are wooled but feel bare skin
freeze and burn with winter's barb.
I wrap and tie and wrap again.

Windy fingers creep and shove,
They poke and pry, "Let me inside!"
They grasp my hands, invade my glove,
probe balled fists I try to hide.

Ewe by ewe, through sorting pen,
we stomp and wave, but mostly huff.
Border collies nip and bend
while guard dogs curl in tail-wrapped ruff.

Horse statues stand with frosted glow,
hair sparkling up like diamond dust—
backs to the wind, heads held low.
Hooves paw the crunchy snowy crust.

Beneath our feet roll icy balls.
manure bits now marble hard
that tease and threaten slippery falls
and make this earth a moving yard.

The pistol shot of sorting gate
and tally cry as sheep make way
straight on to where the pasture waits
to nurture them for one more day

And nurture us, for weeks and years.
This sage and snow marks our fates
while winter's breath, and ours and theirs
rises timeless. Evaporates.

Blown Out—Volados

Oscar calls—

"Las borriegas caminaban ante el viento,
volados." I translate these words in my mind—
"The sheep walked before the wind—blown out."

On the Red Desert, wild country, working land,
the wind blows, and sheep graze, and men tend them.
Sometimes, gales wail, and push the ewes far and far

from their grazing grounds, where each rising and fall,
where each sage-topped and wind-sculpted hill, where
each two-track trail, with rabbit brush and rabbits,

nurtures them. Dunes and draws and each named rim—
Cyclone Rim and Chain Lakes Rim—all the edges,
Siberia Ridge—shelter their known world

most of the time. But those times do come when
the wind is just so, howling in from the West—
or sometimes questing north, and the sheep blow out—

meaning, the ewes walk and walk before it,
no fences to stop their journey, no respite—
winds urging them on, icy blasts at their backs.

"When it blows like this," we warn the shepherds,
"take to your camps, wait, keep the fire ablaze.
The sheep will walk, the storm will pass—then search."

"You can do no more." And they can but wait,
the wind crying out its siren song—Go. Stay.
Are my ewes dead in a draw? Are my dogs warm?

Border collies curl tucked under the wagon,
horses huddle snug in their blankets, tails turned
to the wind, heads held low to the ground while

all wait—men and dogs and horses—the winds
shove and bully. The ewes, heavy with lambs,
walk before the pure force compelling them

forward. The herders, so far from their homes,
so far from their families waiting in Peru,
hear the howling, shiver, cling close to the stove.

Then silence. Saddle and bridle the horses,
whistle up the dogs, then seek faint tracks on the
hard blown snow. Time now to seek after sheep

and pray—and to call the patron saying,
"Las borriegas caminaban ante el viento,
volados." Fortunes lie in the balance.

The Folks

Wind River Dancers, Elk Crossing

Aieee, the cry that soaks bone deep,
an ancient keen disturbs your sleep.

A coyote's howl, an eagle's scream,
a primal call, it haunts your dream

Of times when Old Ones strode this land,
and loved and warred and made their stand.

Ever under the eerie cry,
comes the hum as the drummers try

To pound a sound like thunder's boom,
underlie the cry the singers croon.

Timeless tunes that set the stage,
with grass and sky and scent of sage,

To draw the dancers old and young,
led by song and the rhythmic thrum.

Dancers swoop like birds in flight,
and on their grassy stage alight,

And dance and dive and bow and sway,
ever the music leads their way.

Beads and jangles shine and spark,
swift as hawk, light as lark.

Feathers frame the Shoshoni Rose.
The dancer stamps and hops and knows,

That he follows in his father's step,
who also bowed and jumped and leapt.

The women twirl and swirl and preen,
and rise to meet the lofty keen

Of song and drum, of that sound,
that guides their flight here on the ground.

Beads that sparkle, tins that shine,
buttery buckskin, work so fine—

Winter's work, Grandmother's skill,
beads through skin, threads through quill,

To decorate the dancer's gait,
their prancing steps to illustrate,

Dazzle the eye, and draw the throng,
with light and music, sound and song—

Ever the song, ever the drum,
the pounding pulse of thrum, thrum, thrum.

This step of dance goes deep as bone,
light as bird flight, old as stone.

Shearing at the JO Ranch

In spring, my mother's kitchen bubbled,
while, phone-bound, Dad negotiated dates,
with crew bosses. We awaited the arrival
of strong men armed with sheep shears,
bringing with them good honest hunger.

April brought this most essential of tasks—
a task that called for moving the camps and
trailing the sheep, staging, and shearing,
and the gathering of a motley crew,
assembling at the old JO headquarters.

Mom baked pans of brownies, mounds of rolls,
moist cakes, pyramids of cookies—awaiting
summons to move—lock, stock and cooking pots
to the JO kitchen, with its plank tables,
with its massive wood-burning stove.

Eight years old—an eager assistant,
she trusted me with a knife, chopping nuts,
and onions. Under her eye, I packed dishes,
condiments, seasonings, pans, soap, towels,
preparing to feed an army of appetites.

And preparing me, her number one helper.
My teachers sent stacks of homework,
as I made ready to miss a week of school,
at least. Shearing is an event certain,
but not a date certain. We waited.

We had fresh running water—running
from a sweet spring and piped to the kitchen.
Food kept in the cool room in that stone house—
walls two feet thick. And solid. No need
for a refrigerator behind those rock walls.

We didn't have—electricity,
but lanterns instead, filled outdoors before
dusk, with kerosene. No indoor plumbing—
the outhouse worked fine, though scary at night.
We had a plan. Well, not me, but my parents

Knew how to plan the intricate dance,
the step and pause of bringing sheep, and corrals
and men; mountains of food, ready and canned,
and plates, silverware and dishpans. Plans.
Wool bags, paint, powder and spray. Dog food.

And to bring me--pencils, paper, schoolwork,
Barbie dolls, and Ken, a stuffed puppy, bedroll—
and a flashlight to light my Oz books
after the lanterns' flames were puffed out—
Mom and Dad in the big bed, me on a cot.

When the word came, "The shearers are here!"
we'd unpack all that food—brownies and cookies
still wafting sweet scents, and sweet temptation.
Really, Mom unpacked and organized, prepared.
I assisted—her ready helper, her shadow.

I followed Mom's directions—important,
essential to the team. Dad stacked cordwood
to fuel the great stove where she conjured up
soups, stews, chilis—where huge steaming pots
simmered with potatoes and noodles and rice.

"Sharon, we need you to tromp wool.
Come to the shed after dishes are cleaned up."
I'd follow Dad to the shearing pens
where ewes moved orderly up the chute,
where generators powered machines,
hung overhead, clattering, humming.

26

Men bending, bowing, sweeping long strokes,
powerful arms arcing smooth paths,
wool falling away like orange peels,
and folding itself into packets
swept away, tied up with paper string.

Fleeces tossed up and over, falling into
bags, burlap bags suspended from hoops—
Territory bags they called them, for wool
from the territories, like Wyoming.
Soft balls, needing stomped snug and solid.

Men jumped into the void—compressing
fleeces into compact rolls, set to be tied—
ears at each corner, raw wool stuffing
the tuffed grip, tied off—a handle ready
for the push and roll to a towering stack.

And to think—they needed me—all sixty pounds,
to jump to the bottom of the territory bag,
light at the top of the tunnel, anticipating
each fleece, soft and smelling of lanolin and sage,
tumbling down beneath my feet, to be tromped.

When it was full to the top, someone heavier
might give it the final few stomps just to be sure.
They'd tie off the bag, and roll it away, ready
for the buyers in Boston, and the mills, and the
world beyond—unborn suits, socks, sweaters.

"Good job," Dad praised me, leading me back
to the rock house, warm with cookstove heat,
smelling of wood, and hot water, and old stone.
Mom sat me down, combed my skin for ticks.
Then I'd nap, getting ready for suppertime chores.

Touch and Go

Touch and go—
Red semi tractor, silver trailer,
came all the way from Virginia
to the high desert, Badwater pasture
to haul wool.

Our future depends on
its safe journey to New Mexico,
then on to mills—
fine fibers bound for China
or Italy
or Afghanistan.

Young driver
seeking his way from Honduras,
Following America's roads.

Touch and go—
guiding that big rig
up the muddy two track
from the shearing grounds.

The Ganadero's Lament

Calling Lima, Lima, Lima,
this cry sings out above
the baaing, surging woolies
striving forward—push and shove.

The ding, ding, ding of tin dogs,
bark and nip from flesh and blood,
whoosh and whistle move sheep onward—
they flow, they ebb, they flood.

The corrals that stood in silence
now ring out with urgent noise.
Prods tapping, dogs a'yapping,
"Lima, Lima," comes a voice.

It's a call beyond the clamor,
heard above the coyotes yip,
heard below the raven's caw,
past the snapping crack of whip.

These men name their ancient city,
an echo from their home,
a ganado's destination—
it rings out like a poem.

"Lima, Lima, Lima"
It sings out like a song,
earth and sheep and sky—
the home for which they long.

Just Me
  (For Reba)

Bum lambs cryin'
Lookin' for a mama
Hungry tummies growlin'.
They've only got me.

Cryin' for some warm milk
Hopin' for a little snack
Of somethin' that'll fill 'em up.
They've just got me.

Mixin' up some powder
Warm and lumpy—strained.
Replacer, they call it.
No mama, just me.

Bouncin' 'round my legs
Hopin' for a nuzzle
Just a bucket with some nipples
Filled with milk by me.

No mama cryin' out
For her baby strayin'
Or maybe just out playin'.
Twice a day, they've got me.

Waitin' by the gate
All bones 'n' eyes 'n' tummy
Lookin' for a mama
That they figure is me.

A chore is how I figure it
Can't love 'em—they may die
A scratch behind the ears is all
They'll get from me.

In the house awaitin'
My own babies needin' love
Don't ever want 'em bummed.
They all need me.

Time Was

Time was
the Eureka Pool crew
gathered in June,
cleaned the country of cows,
sorted them by outfit.
trailed from desert
to forest.
In-common, uncommon allotment.

Half-grown kids.
old stone-breakers,
filled up the crew,
but we made hands.
Rode the big circles
swept cattle before us
like dust.
Like time.

Country went on forever
we thought.
Sage and sand and
swivel-necked antelope
marked every direction.
We knew each draw
each crossing
where the Muddy meandered
back on itself.

Jumped horses up
into the old straight truck.
Once the boys
slipped a tire off the dam
three-sixtied into the dry reservoir.
Kenny and Barry soared
shirttails flapping.

from the top of the cab.
Horses picked themselves up
shook off dirt.
Nobody hurt.

Cool dark mornings
we'd mount and mill,
horses snorting, pawing.
Waiting while
Chris and Scott
bucked out their broncs.
"Come on, boys—
We're burnin' daylight!"

The "chh, chh, chh"
of a coiled rattler
curdled sweat.
The sudden thrill
broke the monotony
of following cattle.
Made time stand still.
"Leave her alone—
She might have babies"
my Dad would say.

We'd watch for
dust in the distance.
Mom's lunch truck
sure made the mouth water.
We could smell, taste, know
hot biscuits and stew,
steam rising.
Brownies.
Blessed water.

Woe were we those days
she couldn't find us.
She was a genius to follow

Dad's directions.
"We'll stop by that spring
where Vicente got bucked off
that time."
Cowboys rode miles,
topped the horizon
looking for those brownies.

The day's gather in
the Headquarters Pasture—
we'd load up fresh horses,
make camp for a new circle.
Coyote calls zipping shivers
up and down the spine.
Sagebrush serenade.
Fourteen hours in the saddle.
We sure didn't recite poetry.

Smylie Place Graves

Range cons call it "exclosure"—
this fence grown solid with brush,
sarvisberries, chokecherries, wildflowers,
perennial, but planted there by
their mother.

Homestead children, early deaths—
illness swept them in the day
before vaccine and antibiotics.
Two children, graves still here
hard by our hayfield,

Homestead house long gone.
Dad remembered taking it down—
something about bullets in the walls
from an old shootout.
Home gone, but graves still tended.

If we left this land
who would remember
these children?—
dead a hundred years
or so.

Mustang Man

"I'm a mustang man," he told me
that January night in Elko,
eyes glowing, loving those ponies—
words drawn out by my interest.
Tales I'd heard before
from pony chasers,
wild horse racers—
tracing with words
the curve of their necks,
their strain and their sweat.
The paints and the buckskins—
colors flashing, hooves smashing
through rough and brushy country.
mustangs leading pursuers—
tails flying, men crying out.
Horses and horses, and mustangers,
racing past blinking rabbits,
antelope taking flight,
hawks catching a riser,
to watch the chase.
My father's voice had glowed
with such tales—
how he'd lamed a good horse
to catch a hammer-headed mare—
but what a ride!
I heard the pride.
"This is what I do.
I catch wild horses."
But how?
These days the mustang men
can only ride for the BLM,
managing ponies—
send 'em out to Wyoming.
Then I knew.

He had found a way
to run wild horses,
with benefits.

He Sleeps
        (For Rhen)

He sleeps.
Baby breath against my neck,
worn out from stomping his cowboy boots
on the cookhouse floor,
and hollering "yee-haw"
and "outside".
Soon he'll follow his folks
and the big kids
off on a gentle horse.
But for now,
he sleeps.

In Winter I Can Breathe

In winter I can breathe
without spring's mad rush of anxiety
about trailing and shearing and
explaining to the BLM that
we are doing pretty much the same
as we have done for the
Past Forty Years.

And on the cusp between spring and summer,
the worry, worry, worry of getting
babies on the ground
Alive.

Watching the skies, the thermometer
the Weather Channel, the haystack,
then branding and docking and coyotes
and keeping everyone
Alive.

Then onto the Forest where
bears await,
not afraid of the guard dogs
who are not afraid of them.

And scanning the skies for rain,
waiting for wind and
falling dead trees.
wondering about drought.
Will the feed last until
the off date?
Will fire come
and consume us all?

Then trailing off and finding enough
places to be until the fall work is done.
Sorting mamas from babies,
listening to all that
mooing and baaing, and hoping
the trucks show up on time
and that the roads aren't too icy
as they transport
precious cargo.

Their lives
and ours.
So when the cows
are on winter pasture,
and the ewes are trailed and settled
on the desert,
and the dogs are alert to coyote cries
and the corn pile is high
and the winter winds don't blow too hard,
I can breathe.

The Landscape

Drought, After a Hard Winter

Why do these dry days bake us so
with sun and heat and clear clear skies?
We thought ourselves so weather-wise
when we withstood the chill and blow—

Harsh winter's hand that laid so rough
now turns to show its other side—
roaring snowmelt gone. Now dried
up fields beg water from shovel's sluff

And lift—irrigator's blessed turn
with damming tarps that catch and lead
soothing drops to spread and seep
these turn the field to green from burn.

Miserly spend last season's wealth
to bring us through next winter's stealth.

Hot days will turn and turn again,
as winter seeks earth's slant and spin.

Elijah on the Mount
(For Mr. Sandman of Sandman Mountain)

I invite you, Sandman,
into my bed this night.
Bring with you the fine
ground bits of stone
formed in that whirlwind.

Sweep in as you may.
Seep under the doorframe.
Its solid form cannot hold you back.
Sweep in through slivery cracks
creased by time in window frames.

Settle your fine magic grains
and dust my face with your finest
leavings from the broken rocks,
rent in ages past to test your will
and fill your pack. It is full.

You may leave your mountaintop,
your stony form on its endless climb.
You need not seek tablets of truth,
only relief for my seeking soul,
only bring the blessing of sleep.

Creep into my bed and cover me.
Kiss my eyes with your powdery touch.
Leave only bits of grit
and rock, forgiveness for my
spinning mind, thunderous thoughts,

Quiet these fires, this trembling.
Leave me the peace of slumber,
I who am most in need of rest.

Come down from your mount.
Sandman, come to me tonight.

1 Kings 19:5
And as he lay and slept under a juniper tree, behold, then an angel touched
him....

1 Kings 19:11
And he said, Go forth, and stand upon the mount before the LORD. And,
behold, the LORD passed by, and a great and strong wind tore the
mountains, and broke in pieces the rocks before the LORD; but the LORD
was not in the wind: and after the wind an earthquake; but the LORD was
not in the earthquake:

Eureka Pool, Spring Gather

Each June,
we gathered winter cattle
off the Eureka Pool,
desert ranch—
took two weeks.
We rode the big circles—
sorted pairs by brand
and wattle,
trailed on to mountain pastures
glimmering on the horizon.

Red Flat, so far out—
took an hour just to ride across.
The old railroad tie stockade,
winter windbreak,
its only landmark.
Hard to imagine
those hot shining days,
cows huddled stony
before a blizzard.

Haystack Mountains
mounded up like a teamster's
bad dream,
creased the horizon.
The Flat Tops
set the southern arc
of our circle,
sundial sweeping the marks.

The country rolled away.
Barrel Spring—
where we drowsed and
 saddlehorses drank,
Eureka headquarters,

where round corral
stubs still beckoned—
the past shimmering
just there.

Tiger Hill—
"slicker than tiger shit!"
when the track turned muddy.
The old Dew Place—
Bachelor George made cowboys
kick off their boots,
kept a clean floor.

Dad Station—
haunted by ghosts:
Overland stage drivers,
sweating, blowing teams.
Their dust still rises.

Muddy Creek
cut the country,
gathered water,
meandered and moved on
down to the Colorado,
as we followed cows
and the days slid away—
hourglass sands sifting
downstream.

Marked country—
two track roads,
artesian water,
earth-bermed dikes.
game trails and
stock trails and
stage trails and
the Eureka crew
trailing cattle.

One or two gas wells
drowsed on the horizon,
like scouts,
like seeds.
How could we know?
the world would turn,
wells spreading,
settling
like fine-blown grit,
like fallen stars.

Country's still there.
Barrel Springs
and Eureka
name roads and wells,
rigs and pipelines.
Men roiling the country
can't tell you the name
of that rim right there
where we chased antelope
who left us, contemptuous,
in their dust.

Ghost Steps

Wet snow covers dead fall grasses,
and we lay down ghost footprints
as the heavy step of boots
treads down a frozen outline
preserved as layers and layers
of snowfall deepen into cold.

Those first frosty footsteps
of the season lie like spirits
throughout the long dark cold times
that pass. Months when hidden ground
is covered, protected—when sound
is muffled and softened and dim.

Finally, the sun swings north,
winter's snow dissolves and runs
in rivulets, soaks into ground,
drawn toward thaw by the season—
spring's exorcism at long last.
Now from beneath winter's cover

Appears all forgotten debris
concealed by winter's blanket,
autumn's forgotten treasures—
faded toys, gnawed bones, sodden leaves
and the apparition of those
ghost steps, laid down long ago.

Horizon's Edge

Mountains slice horizon's edge,
purple stones that cut sky's blue
with climbing, crumbling ancient ledge,
bisecting earth and heav'n in two.
With rock-cut boundaries sharp and clean,
clear sky lies nigh on landscape's glow,
two realms with nothing in between—
just blurry blend of earth and snow.
No mist where sea slides into sky—
No foggy realm where edge dissolves—
No script "Beyond here monsters lie"—
No doubt where edge of map resolves.

The earth ends here, just here you see—
horizon's edge, eternity.

Hunger Moon

Winter solstice, Red Desert moon lies new, a shimmering wink
glancing through this sundown gloom, reflected gleam, a slender blink.

Slide away, sun's last glow, faded rose. Shine on new moon,
illuminate sky's crystal snow, floating, drifting, gemstones strewn

through night. This season, winter well and truly here, now come to pass,
time to cast its long dark spell. Wax and wane, wane and wax.

This circle dance, the moon is full. Hunger moon, it gleams and shines.
on desert snow, on draw and hill. Antelope mill, try to find

summer's grass 'neath drift and sage. Wild horses nose and paw.
Elk break through snow's crust and gage each blown off ridge, each
drifted draw.

The world turns back, it rolls along, indifferent to this starving time.
No sense of right, no feel of wrong, 'til sun and moon, 'til stars align,

until sage sea feels the pull, brings equinox to season's fore.
Shine on spring moon, grown fat and full.

Draw life to this Red Desert shore.

New Year's Blank Slate

The year dawns new
and clean
and full of hope.
Sunrise sending
gleams of light sparkling
across snowy meadows,
shining up like
diamond shards—
crystal glimmers pricking
the frosting spread
smooth across the fields.
In spring, these hills hide
baby calves with mama cows
mooing softly.
Summer hums with
growing hay, and tractors
rolling past midnight,
directed by dew upon
moonlit windrows.
Autumn brings lambs,
deer, elk, grazing on
harvest's aftermath.
Then the long brown
quiet awaits
snow, and silence
and the shimmering
pallet waiting for sunrise,
Painting the
New Year.

Old Man Winter

Hot summer days don't fool me.
Old man winter, I see you.
You lurk, sending sunrises a little later
each morning,
and the promise of frost
whispering to the dew on the grass.

Sweat rolls down my spine,
but I know
wool socks and snowboots await me.
Moonrises over snowfields
will make the nights glow.
Whoever said you were an old man
anyway?

Red Desert Sojourn

Sharp hooves chip through icy drifts,
trudging feet that fall and lift,
carve out a path and stomp and go,
a narrow line through frozen snow.

The claxon call of pickup horn
brings sheep to seek the proffered corn.
Kernels glow, sweet gold on white,
to ease their hunger, winter plight,

And nurture lambs which grow within
warm and wet, placental skin.
Mothers wear their raw wool coats
and winds without howl Arctic notes.

This winter sun slowly arcs
cross southern sky to early dark.
Land smothered still in snowy pall,
no note is heard, spring's siren call.

Ewes stomp and stand and paw and know
they'll bear the pass of chill and blow,
bear these months of dark and drift,
of snows that churn and rise and sift.

They'll eat the corn, they'll graze the sage
til April brings them longer days
and warmth and sun and blessed grass,
and bitter winter's days have passed.

For eons past, and still to come,
primeval memories of sun
sustain them through this ice and cold,
sustains us all, these lives we hold.

Water Witchery

Watching the witch conjure up water,
magic of the most powerful kind,
performing before our very eyes
this most essential mystical rite—
feeling through dirt and rock and sand,
fossil water, interred long ago.

The ancient waterways still wending
a way beneath the earth, with memories
of birds, and fish, the smell of burnt lightening—
rain driving down upon the earth,
becoming river, or pond, or pounding waves
crashing on primeval shores.

The branches newly cut, raw wound
still marking the break from the living bush—
fruit-bearing only—chokecherry, sarvisberry—
a fertile bough now seeking to heed
a beckoning from dark waters below—
waters, summoned, which strive to rise.

Waters calling to the supple stem
now drawn to hear the siren song,
unheard by those deaf to its refrain—
the subtle ripple far below
which only sings to those who know,
who feel the spell of water.

The witch calls upon the cosmos
to guide the boughs crossed like lovers
pulled together unheeding—
the powerful draw compelling
the water below and the branch above
beguiling each other inexorably.

This powerful gift comes to those
who claim it as a birthright
and learn the ways of boughs and damp.

"Yup, it's about three hundred feet down,
about fifteen gallons per minute,"
he prophesies, reading our fortune.

'Round the Campfire

The Sage Grouse Strut

It's the Sage Grouse strut.
It's the Sage Grouse stroll.
It's the Sage Grouse hustle.
We boys are on a roll.

To impress our feathered friends,
we puff and shoot the breeze,
hootin', "Hey there, ladies—
you're some fancy chickadees!"

 I can thrust my chest out—
like two shiny pearly shields.
I can waggle spotted tail feathers
in these sagebrush springtime fields.

I can flap my grousey wings
with a fancy dancey fly—
that bird with ruffled plumage
can't even flutter to the sky.

"Hey girls, look here at Big Bird!
Do you like what you see?
I'm the coolest guy out here.
Hey darlin' chickies, pick me!

"Just smell that spicy sagebrush,
(you can quit your hiding place).
The hen party should be over.
It's me you should embrace!

"You may be small and brown,
but you're winsome as can be.
Shake your bootie over here
and make some eggs with me.

"Just ignore that moulty bird
with his wimpy rooster tail.
Take a brushy stroll with me
along this sagey trail.

"I'm a'stompin' and a'struttin'
upon this crowded lek.
Forget your frumpy henfriends—
I'm at your call and beck.

"I'm the coolest cockerel—
see that rooster over there
can hardly puff his chest out.
He's only suckin' air.

"That chicken who's paradin'
and a'prancin' through the sage
couldn't hardly get a date
if he was dancin' on a stage,

"And that struttin' fool you see
is nothin' but a poult.
If you study him real close
he's about to start to moult!

"Don't even take a look—
that cocky dude is not the best.
He'll love ya and he'll leave ya
with chicks tucked in the nest.

"Just ignore those other birds,
with their inferior display.
I'm the ace who offers
the best sort of DNA.

"I'm the best grouse on the lek.
I'm a struttin' fool, you see—
so take the Sage Grouse stroll
through the scented brush with me!

"It's the Sage Grouse strut.
It's the Sage Grouse dance.
Step right up, you sexy hen—
It's time for Grouse romance!"

Help Wanted

Oh Lord, please bring our ranch a cook—
one who dazzles with great food,
who makes it all from soup to nuts—
who fills our every hungry want,
who's quick of wit and quick of hand,
one whom all our needs will fill!

It's more than bellies needing filled—
more than foodstuffs needing cooked
We need a cook who'll "make a hand"
and sanely turn out fragrant food.
Sanity is what we want.
to keep the boss from going nuts.

It's a fact most cooks are nuts.
Ask restaurateurs with jobs to fill.
A steady chef is all they want,
I say "no chefs, it's just cooking."
On the table, we need good food
to fill up all our hungry hands.

Ranchwork gives them roughened hands.
Salt of the earth, now they're not nuts.
Hard work makes them pile their food
high, with seconds their plates are filled.
It's rice and meats, and greens need cooked
and sweets to fill their hungry wants.

At our table, we know no want.
We've honest work to turn our hands.
Is it too much to want a cook
who's nice and steady, and not nuts?!
Of crazy cooks, I've had my fill,
I'm full up, no need for food!

Mem'ries flood, give food
for thought. A stable cook is all I want!
With hungry bellies needing filled
I really, really need a hand
with food and drink, from soup to nuts.
Is that too much to ask a cook?

It takes food to fill our hands,
I pray for one who is not nuts,
Who'll fill our needs, this perfect cook!

Baggs, Cowtown of the West

Between the river and the road,
lies a little place that's know'd
as Baggs, Wyoming, Cowtown of the West.
Rough and tumble, rough and ready,
rough and tough, folks there hold steady
to the Code of the West. It's stood the test.

George Baggs and his wife Maggie
settled there upon this craggy
rugged place to raise their cows and settle down.
Next the gamblers and the sports
and all stripes of other sorts
stopped there too, and soon Baggs became a town.

Outlaws roamed about the street.
Why, Chick Bowen chanced to meet
Bad Bob Meldrum, who then just shot him dead.
Local folks, they made no fuss
at events that happened thus.
"Hope he didn't mess the streets," is all they said.

When Butch Cassidy with his gang
stopped and robbed the UP train,
they headed right to Baggs with all their loot.
Flush with all their pillage,
Baggs was the choicest village
to spend their gains and drink and ride and shoot.

This town had a reputation
where one could cause sensation,
where local folks were tolerant and kind.
A cowtown through and through,
that's what everybody knew—
a more Western burg would be hard to find.

And just outside of town
rich pastures could be found,
precious water—an herbivore's delight.
Deer and elk, and cows and sheep,
they all graze to earn their keep—
both then and now, they offer quite a sight.

In the summer, they all pass
to the mountains, green with grass.
They must move up to find their summer feed.
In the winter, comes the snow,
to the desert, they must go,
each way, right through the streets, they must proceed.

Now for years, it's been the way,
on the livestock trailing day,
for town folks to step out and lend a hand.
As the cattle trotted through,
they might push a calf or two,
or help along a moving ovine band.

All the stock hands came along
to control their cowy throng,
to see their charges safely through the place.
They'd surround 'em, it is true,
but some rebels would slip through,
and lead their keepers on a merry chase.

The cowboys did their darndest
to keep those bovines harmless,
to keep an outlaw cow from a stampede.
"We don't know what the fuss is.
We don't want to raise a ruckus.
Be patient as they pass, is all we plead."

In recent times, we've seen a change,
as the livestock when they range
hit the town like Butch Cassidy and his boys.

The cows' manners while in town
made leading citizens all frown.
Cow poop upon the streets, it sure annoys.

Just now Baggs has made the news.
and local folks have aired their views.
In Baggs, it's gettin' Western once again.
There's a modern range war battle,
but it's not sheep and cattle.
The fight is man versus beast, that is plain.

For some cattle ran amok,
leaving cow hands out of luck.
They chased and raced their charges through the town.
The Wild Bunch had come back.
Lawns and gardens were ransacked.
They turned the streets of Baggs quite upside down.

Oh, the cow folks cried the hardest
as they dashed after their charges—
dogs a yappin', town folks flappin' at the fray.
Pots and pans, they were a'bangin',
why we thought there'd be a hangin'.
'fore those cows got out of town on that long day.

There were dogs a'chasin' 'round,
a cacophony of sound,
as town folks tried to save their greenery.
"We sure aren't very fond
of these cows upon our lawn.
Marauders don't improve the scenery."

List'ners heard a lot of yelling
as the gardeners were telling
those nasty beasts not to destroy their lawn and seed.
In the end, they had a roundup—
got those cows fin'lly through town, yup.
At last the cowboys halted the stampede.

Those Baggs folks had a powwow,
said, "We've got to stop these cows, now—
teach 'em manners, make 'em stay right where they should."
Next they called up the town father—
said, "We want to stop this bother.
This trail through town, it isn't any good!"

They sent a firmly worded letter,
told the livestock folks they'd better
follow paths, and also rules they must obey.
If ranchers want to trail through town,
their name and number must go down
on a permit, to give their rights away.

Well, the ranchers were aghast
at this unexpected blast,
from Baggs, Wyoming, Cowtown of the West.
They were chaffin' at the bit—
said, "We won't sign no permit.
It's our right to trail, and we just do our best."

"Why, without the ranchin' folk,
there'd be no town, no joke,
It's the cows that built this town, don'cha know.
Oil field jobs might bring a buck,
but next year you're out of luck,
as they plug their wells, and take their jobs and go."

The town board called all to meet,
for there'd been less light than heat.
A solution to their problem, they desired.
Baggs folks wanted some persuasion,
and no more bovine invasion.
Perhaps more regulation was required?

Then the livestock man whose cattle
had started up the battle,
apologized and swallowed all his pride.

Said he needed more assistance
for his cows to go the distance.
Next time, he'd bring more cowhands to the ride.

The council then debated
the new rules they had created,
and decided that the current laws would do.
Then they shook hands all around,
in Baggs, a real cowtown,
it's legal now for cattle passing through.

Folks are tolerant and kind,
and a ruckus, they don't mind.
Their Western hospitality's the best.
Passers through they'll warmly greet,
if they don't defile the street!
in Baggs, Wyoming, Cowtown of the West.

Llama Drama

We saw lots of llama drama at the shearing shed tonight,
Mama Beulah and Maria put up a worthy fight.

"Can't you see it's cold out? Can't you see our frosty breath?
It's not weather fit for shearing! No fleece could bring our death!"

"We have barns to give you shelter. We have cozy straw for bed.
There will be no frozen llamas! You have no need for dread."

"But we can see those rams who have lost their wooly coats.
They no longer look majestic. They look more like hairy goats."

"Step right up here, ladies, to the Ladder Ranch salon.
Soon you'll sport the latest style. Your wavy locks will soon be gone."

"No, we like our flowing locks. We like it long and swirly,
We like it warm and thick. Our best look is llama curly."

"Your new look will be most stylish. Your new look will be most sleek.
You'll have the latest, greatest 'dos. Your llama glamour all will
seek."

"Whoa, what is all this racket? What is this clank and clatter?
We don't want a crew cut haircut! Our opinion doesn't matter?!"

"Never mind those four strong guys. Just ignore that noisy shearer.
Lie right down here on the platform. There's no need for fear here."

"Wait, I'm on my back now! You've stretched me stem to stern!
Those blades are sharp upon my skin! Are you sure that it won't burn?"

"Don't struggle so, my llama. Soon this shearing will be done.
From your fleece you'll soon be parted, and your hide will soon see
sun."

"No—I won't take this lying down. It will make this llama sad.
Why, this humiliation just makes me spitting mad!"

"Now you can look just lovely with your new stylish trendy 'do,
You can join your sheep friends, with a cut that's cute and new!"

"No, I don't want this summer haircut! Can't you tell that it's still cold!
I don't like those noisy clippers. I don't like this strongarm hold!"

"We can let her go now. Her shearing is complete.
Oh, yuck! What is this vile goo that's spattered on my feet?!"

"That's my mama llama spit. You deserve that sticky blast.
Maybe next year you'll remember, and this trim will be my last!"

Yup, it was lots of llama drama at the Ladder Ranch tonight.
If you don't mind a little spit—they're quite the stylish sight!

Riding Rough Stock

The rough stock waits in the chute.
Riders tug, straighten their chaps,
screw down their hats, squint and gauge
the critters they aim to ride.

"Now, folks" chants the announcer,
"The third go-round, Mutton Busting.
The riders are six and under,
weighing less than fifty pounds."

Tears flow as a young rider
hugs tight to his father's leg,
snuffles into the dusty denim.
"Cowboy up!" A brave nod.

A brother and sister—busters both—
adjust the numbers pinned to
their shirts, tug at the safety vests,
exchange cowboy hats for helmets.

This is serious business.
The rider drops onto the back
of the ewe with the wary look.
This isn't her first rodeo.

Some grab the bucking strap
snugged behind her front legs—
a handhold on the shorn sheep.
Some wrap their arms around her neck.

"Let me tell you about this critter,"
blares from speakers overhead.
"She's known as Baaaaad Bessie—
and she's never been ridden!"

The rider swallows, and nods,
and the chute gate flies open!
The ewe bolts like lightening
spies the white line dusted in the dirt,

And jumps! The youngster tilts
and turns, seeking mom, or dad,
and grips harder on every wooly bit.
The ground looks hard.

Then *boom*, the dirt rises up,
grit fills teeth, nose and eyes,
suddenly flooded with tears.
The crowd cheers, and claps.

Angelic, the Rodeo Queen appears,
smelling sweet—with hugs and smiles,
and a salute to bravery,
with a dollar bill, a shiny ribbon.

The mutton buster remembers
how the bronc riders do it,
brushes off the dirt and the tears,
and waves to the crowd.

Unanswered Prayers

I was desperate for a ranch cook—
the last one ran away.
We had lots of hungry ranchhands
needin' three meals a day.

I raised my eyes to heaven
with a solemn reverent look.
"Please, dear Lord," I implored,
"Send me a good ranch cook!"

"I don't care if she's crazy.
I don't care if she's lame.
I don't care if she's a he,
or assuming a fake name."

Sometimes the Lord will hear us
when we send up a prayerful plea,
for just then the phone rang
and the caller asked for me!

It was the local preacher.
He said he'd take a chance
to inquire if we needed
a new cook upon our ranch.

"It's the answer to my prayers,"
I told the startled Father.
"Tell her she can come today,'
if it isn't any bother."

"I'll call her right away," he said,
"but she's a stranger here, you see."
"Don't worry," I said firmly,
"She's the answer to my plea,

"For the camptender's in Peru,
and the cowboy quit yesterday.
We already were short-handed
before the old cook ran away!"

I didn't ask for references.
I didn't read her resume.
"She can come today," I told him.
"I need her right away!"

It was nearly noon
When she pulled into the drive.
I sent up a prayer of thanks.
She'd made it here alive!

I thought, "She can set the table.
She can cut the cake—
help me to get his meal on,
because I'm running late."

But—all that set was her
down upon a chair,
while she cast a doubtful look
at the chaos reigning there.

Hungry ranch hands hit the door.
Dinner was in high gear.
They piled full their plates
and food began to disappear.

But—she disappeared too.
By the time that I looked up
I found she'd gone outside again,
and was sitting in her truck.

Her demeanor was distraught.
Her look was one of gloom.
"I don't think that I can stay," she said.
"There isn't enough room."

"What do you mean?" I queried.
"The cookhouse is all yours.
The guys will help you unload your gear
when they're done with all their chores."

She looked at me with sadness.
"Oh, my problem isn't that!
I don't think that it is big enough
for me and all my cats!"

This was not what I expected so
I looked into her truck.
I saw felines everywhere—
furry critters run amok!

Calicos and tiger stripes,
browns and blacks and grays—
a Persian with a pedigree—
a whole camper full of strays!

At this moving mass of felines,
I stared. I swallowed hard.
"Perhaps you're right," I told her.
"Go this way to leave the yard."

This made me see the wise words
By country star Garth Brooks.
"Thank the Lord for Unanswered Prayers"
can apply, as well, to cooks!

Author's Biography

Sharon Salisbury O'Toole is a rancher, writer, and poet. Her family has stewarded the same landscape in the Little Snake River Valley, along the Wyoming-Colorado border, since 1881. She and her husband, Patrick; daughter, Meghan; and son, Eamon, operate the Ladder Ranch. They raise cattle, sheep, horses, dogs, and children. An urban daughter, Bridget, is also a writer.

Sharon has a degree in Technical Journalism from Colorado State University. She is a journalist who writes mainly about the West, natural resources, and the issues which affect agriculture and food production. She writes a monthly column for The Shepherd magazine and has had essays and editorials published in newspapers and magazines nationwide. She has had two children's books about ranch life published by Scholastic.

Sharon is an award-winning poet. She has performed at the National Cowboy Poetry Gathering in Elko, Nevada; the Trailing of the Sheep Festival in Ketchum, Idaho; and other events, especially those at the Little Snake River Museum in Savery, Wyoming. She also writes "Ranch News", a blog about life on their ranch at www.ladderranch.com.

www.reddashboard.com

Made in the USA
San Bernardino, CA
06 February 2020

64112781R00058